THE
ROAD CYCLIST'S
COMPANION

BY PETER DRINKELL

cicada

KIT 6
BIB SHORTS 11
JERSEY 17
HELMET 19
SHOES AND SOCKS 21
ACCESSORIES 23
BEING PREPARED 27

BIKE FIT 34
SETTING UP YOUR CLEATS 37
SIZE AND SADDLE 39
REACH AND HANDLEBARS 43
FRAME GEOMETRY 45
FRAME OPTIONS 49

GROUP RIDING 54
DRAFTING 58
HAND SIGNALS 63
GENERAL GROUP RIDE 67
SINGLE PACELINE 71
ROTATING PACELINE 77
CYCLOSPORTIVES AND ROAD RACING 79

TECHNIQUE 84
PEDALLING 88
GEARING 91
DESCENDING 95
BRAKING 101
BUNNY HOPS 105

TRAINING 106
ENERGY 111
FUNDAMENTALS OF TRAINING 119
MOSTABILITY AND STRETCHING 129
FUELLING AND HYDRATION 135

Cycling can be a minefield to the uninitiated. There are literally thousands of unwritten rules – from the length of your socks to the 'luft' of your cap to the nuances of behaviour when cycling in a group. Most of these mysteries are uncovered when riding for a club from an early age – learning by rote from the elders, who pass their knowledge (often impatiently) down the chain.

My first experiences of road riding were an individual endeavour, training for triathlons at the age of 18. Clipless pedals were only just emerging on the market (it was the mid '80s), so there I was, strapped into my toe clips, killing myself on climbs, grinding out mile after mile, not really sure what I was doing. My only tutors were worn out training manuals and avidly watched repeats of the Giro and the Tour de France. Not having a foundation in club cycling meant that I missed some of the crucial aspects of technique and etiquette that probably could have made my journey a whole lot easier. As it was, I learned the hard way, with some cracking errors of judgment on everything from training to apparel *en route*.

I have to give my thanks to two people who helped me wake up to the finer joys of group riding; firstly to my brother-in-law Mike Bigmore, who was a great help as I became more serious about my cycling ambitions, guiding me through the nuanced world of cycling kit and shouting at me for half-wheeling him – not that I had any clue what he was talking about. Secondly, to my friend, Mark Neep, owner of cycle travel company GPM10. I got involved with his company firstly as a photographer, and later helping as a guide on the training camps. It was on these trips that I really learnt the skill of group riding, and an appreciation for the rules. Working with inexperienced riders makes you realise that some of the seemingly insignificant mannerisms and traditions actually fulfill a crucial function in preserving the safety of the group, as well as a sense of togetherness.

After 15 years of cycling in groups, I am still by no means a perfect cyclist, and it's thanks to Mike and Mark laughing at me for all the mistakes I made and go on making that I came up with the idea for this book. If I take a harsh tone in some places, you'll have to forgive me – the world of cycling is not always entirely tolerant, and you'll find your co-riders in many groups taking a similarly abrasive approach. Try not to take offence – one of the joys of road cycling is that underneath it all there's an essential acceptance and respect of one another, as you all work together to make the ride enjoyable.

KIT

Group cycling is all about the group. If you're a runner, you can wear whatever you like – it's just you after all. But the culture of cycling is much more nuanced. By wearing the 'right' clothes, you are effectively showing respect to your group-mates. You are conveying a readiness to follow the rules, to work for a more enjoyable group ride, in which everyone takes turns and follows the etiquette to make the paceline function efficiently. So yes, you can show up wearing baggy shorts and a string vest, but to be honest, you're going to get given an uncomfortably wide berth by everyone else in the group, which somewhat defeats the purpose.

Wearing the right kit on the bike is not necessarily going to make you a better or stronger rider, but it will make you look the part and that is a very important factor on the road.

Tight, figure hugging clothing is the order of the day. Lycra is more aerodynamic and is worn by the pros. In truth, for the amateur rider, although Lycra may marginally improve your performance on a time trial course or downhill, it will make no difference on those long slow climbs. The real benefits are that Lycra is durable, doesn't chafe, is flexible and dries quickly. And, of course, it makes you look pro.

If you are not that great a rider and you look the part, people will just think you are having a bad day. Have a bad day and not look the part and people will just think you are a bad rider.

Having said that, there is room for interpretation, and what you wear on the bike can be a very personal thing in some respects. The key is, however you choose to dress, make sure all your kit – jersey, shorts, socks, cap, helmet etc., matches. The following pages will help you navigate the intricacies of how to wear what on a bike. Some of these 'rules' are for functional reasons, and others are purely aesthetic.

Clean lines, kit matching and a tight fit are the all important factors.

Your bib shorts are probably your most important item of clothing. For men, simple padded shorts are out of the question. Bib shorts only. This isn't just to look good but to prevent movement and unnecessary chafing when you're spending hours in the saddle. Bibs offer a lot more support, holding the padded chamois in place and reducing movement of the clothing, without reducing movement of the body. They have more fabric around your back and mid-section, which protects you from the elements when taking a more extreme aero position, and also provides coverage if your jersey moves around – after all, nobody wants to follow a wheel with a builder's crack in their face.

THINGS TO PAY ATTENTION TO WHEN BUYING BIB SHORTS

Fit: Your bibs should be figure hugging. Common sense prevails here; not so tight as to restrict blood flow and threaten your chance of ever reproducing, but tight enough so that your shorts don't flap in the wind or bunch up in all the wrong places.

Chamois: The padded chamois in the crotch is there for both comfort and hygiene, drawing sweat away from your skin so you don't overheat. To work effectively, it should be a close fit with your skin. The thickness of the padding is variable between brands and styles and is a matter of personal preference. Try them on, ideally on your bike, and see how they feel. On a long ride, the chamois will make the difference between comfort and excruciating pain. A chamois cream (or nappy cream) will also help reduce friction.

Straps: If the straps on your bibs tug at your shoulders, it's a sign they are too small. Bibs are cut to be worn in the ride position, not standing up, so when testing, take the ride position to see how they feel. In this position the straps may not tug at your shoulders.

Legs: Some bib shorts are longer in the leg than others. It is important that the seam of the leg of your bibs lines up in the same place on your leg, so that you keep your tan lines sharp. You may have to fold up the gripper of the leg to make them perfectly line up. Those tan lines are your evidence of long hours in the saddle.

Bib tights: During winter you would use bib tights. Generally these do not have a chamois and go over your bib shorts to keep you warm. You can get bib tights with a chamois as well, but it goes without saying that you don't want to double up your chamois.

FURTHER BIB SHORT ETIQUETTE

- Make sure your bibs are on the right way round!
- The straps of your bibs go under your jersey and generally over a base layer.
- Never wear underwear under your bibs. They will absorb sweat and increase your risk of chafing.
- Bib shorts should be black. If not black then they should be team issue from the team you ride for, or a training camp you have been on. No white bibs. Wet, dirty, white Lycra bibs leave little to the imagination and are wrong on many levels.
- Don't ever wear running or football shorts over your bibs or tights. Ever.
- Bibs should always have a chamois in them. Shorts or tights direct to skin will do you no favours at all.
- Your shorts always need to be clean – change them every day. Your chamois is designed to have antibacterial qualities but it can't compete with the sweat and grime of a day in the saddle. If you are touring or on an extended trip, take multiple pairs and wash them in the sink when you need to. They will generally dry overnight.
- No old, worn out bib shorts. Nobody wants to be staring at a bum crack through microns of see-through Lycra.
- No bib shorts at breakfast. When on training camps, always come down in your civvies and change after you've eaten.

From top left:
Yellow Jersey: Worn by the leader of the general classification in the Tour de France.
Green Jersey: Worn by the leader of the points competition in the Tour de France.
Polka Dot Jersey: Worn by the 'King of the Mountains' in the Tour de France
Rainbow Jersey: Worn by the winner of the World Championships
National Championship Jersey: This one is worn by the winner of the Belgian National Champs

JERSEY

Cycling jerseys are made from a light, breathable material that wicks well (draws moisture away from your skin), and is engineered for comfort. It should be close fitting, so that it doesn't cause friction or flap in the wind, and so that you get those all important clean lines. When trying it on, it's best to take the ride position to get a feel for the fit. When standing, the jersey might be a little loose, but when your hands are on the bars of your bike, it should fit snugly around your upper back and shoulders.

A cycling jersey will have three pockets at the back for carrying things like inner tubes, phone, money, food for your ride, a rain cape or gilet for when the weather changes. This is so that you don't have to carry a bag on your back (not acceptable at any time). When filling your jersey pockets, distribute things evenly, so it looks neat and there are no bulges to one side. If you're only taking something small, put it in the central pocket.

Jerseys have to have sleeves; short in summer and long in winter. Do not even consider sleeveless jerseys. These are the domain of triathletes, and that still doesn't make them right. Don't roll up the sleeves of your jersey. You want your tan lines to be as crisp and sharp as possible.

Your jersey is your chance to express yourself a little. You can display some colour, and if it is team issue, then your sponsorship. There is much debate in the world of road riding about how acceptable it is to wear pro team or trade team kit if you do not ride with that team. As a purist, I would argue against it, but it doesn't really matter. What does matter is that you respect it. Don't mix team kit – I've seen riders with Astana bib shorts and an HTC Highroad Jersey – everything about that is wrong. Also, don't go overboard – if you're wearing team kit, don't wear the full ensemble. You'll just look like a numpty.

Finally, steer well clear of classification jerseys; yellow jersey, polka dot jersey, rainbow jersey, etc (see left). These jerseys deserve respect and need to be earned.

HELMET

Gone are the days when it looked pro not to wear a helmet. Helmets make basic sense, and you'd struggle to find a pro today who doesn't wear one.

A helmet is not just for protecting the top of your skull, but your face as well. It might not stop a bit of road rash, but if worn properly, it will prevent you from breaking your nose or crushing your cheek. To do its job to best effect, it needs to fit properly and not move around. It should be sitting forward enough to protect the forehead – around two finger widths from your eyebrows – never tilted back. The strap needs to be snug without digging into your throat.

While out riding on a guided trip, I once saw a rider's fork snap, sending him head over handlebars. He hit the tarmac face first, and then bounced into the oncoming traffic, resulting in a motorbike clipping his head coming the other way. The helmet was in pieces, but he only suffered a mild concussion, a split lip and a cut above the eye from his glasses. Had he not been wearing a helmet, the fall would probably have been fatal.

HELMETIQUETTE

- Don't wear your helmet back to front!
- When you are not on your bike, don't hang your helmet on the brake hoods, the drops of your bars or the saddle. Always hang your helmet from the stem. The chinstrap goes around the stem and the lid hangs over the centre of the bars face down. This not only keeps it secure but also neat and symmetrical.
- Don't leave your helmet on when you are sitting in a cafe.
- If your helmet came with a visor attached, ditch it. Visors are for mountain bikers, not road cyclists.

Your road shoes are designed to work with clipless pedals (the name is a little bit deceptive – referring to the toe clips of the old style pedals that were replaced in the '80s when the click-in technology of ski boots was applied to bikes). A cleat is attached to the bottom of the shoe, and this clips into the pedal, holding your foot in place. The sole of the shoe is made of a light, rigid material such as carbon fibre, limiting the movement of your feet, and channelling your power directly into the pedals.

If you've never used clipless pedals before, make sure you practice on a quiet stretch of road, preferably with a grass verge. It won't take long to get the hang of it, but there might be a few comedy moments when you stop and forget to unclip, triggering a slow topple. Once you're used to it, try and stay clipped in as long as possible. Don't clip out 50 metres from the lights in preparation, wait until the second before stopping if you can.

Your socks should be cycle specific socks – which are designed to wick moisture away from the skin, preventing rubbing and reducing the chance of blisters, as well as offering support for your feet.

SHOE TIPS

- Road shoes are designed for cycling – limit the amount of walking you do in them.
- Don't suffer shoe confusion – no mountain bike shoes and certainly no running shoes.

SOCK TIPS

- Socks should cover your ankle and sit below the calf. Never wear football socks, socks that come up over your calves (that includes calf guards or compression socks), or socks that sit below the ankle.
- Keep your socks clean of chain oil and other nasties.
- Some would go as far as to say that socks should be white only. To my mind it doesn't matter as long as it matches your kit.

CAPS

A cotton cycling cap is a great accessory under your helmet and looks very pro. Of course, being cotton, it sort of goes against all the principles of the high tech fabrics that the rest of your kit is made of, but it's very effective at keeping the sweat from dripping into your eyes on hot days and super-human mountain climbs. The small peak can be worn both up and down to shield the eyes from the sun when required. It also keeps a bald head protected from the summer sun and the winter winds. And to be honest, it looks pretty cool when you take your helmet off for that coffee stop.

GLASSES

Your glasses need to be cycling specific, not your aviators. There are practical reasons for this, the lenses are not glass and they are designed not to shatter, lacerating your face if you crash. Also, the lenses are generally interchangeable so you can swap them in different weather conditions.

- Glasses really should be worn at all times on the bike to protect your eyes from flying debris, sun and rain.
- The arms of your glasses should always go over the straps of your helmet, not under.

GLOVES

Gloves are a personal choice. The pros very rarely wear them while out training, but I wear them at all times to protect hands from road rash in case of a fall. In winter full-finger gloves are a necessity, and in summer, fingerless gloves or mitts.

One of the main things to consider when going out for a ride is the weather, and how to prepare for it. As the saying goes, there is no such thing as bad weather, just bad clothing choices. If you bring the right gear you can go out no matter what the weather. This doesn't mean that you have to drag all your kit out on every ride – but use common sense.

A good piece of advice I was once given was 'dress for where you are going, not where you are starting'. If you are heading up into the high mountains, take into account that it might get cold up there. Likewise, if the weather forecast predicts 30 degrees, it's best to brave the early morning cold and dress light. The key is having removable layers that are easy to take off and stow in the pockets of your jersey.

RAIN JACKET / WIND JACKET

A rain jacket is heavier than a wind jacket and more waterproof. If it looks like a really wet, cold day, you should wear a rain jacket, as you probably won't be taking it off for the duration of the ride. If the weather is just windy and/or cold, with a smaller chance of rain or showers, or if you're climbing high into the mountains, I would suggest taking a wind jacket, which is made of lighter fabric and can easily be stowed in your jersey pocket. Some riders stick newspaper under their jerseys to protect their chests on the descents.

GILET

A gilet is a sleeveless vest with a full-length zip made of a breathable fabric. This is one piece of kit that I could not do with out. During spring and autumn, the gilet is always stowed in the back pocket. It's great on cold mornings, in the mountains or on chilly descents. It keeps the wind off your chest while leaving your arms exposed so they don't overheat. It's also an extra layer to add to your arsenal in winter.

A base layer, especially in the winter months, is an essential part of your kit. Sweat cools you down and moisture on your skin will make you cold. Base layers work by drawing the moisture away and keeping you dry.

For it to work to best effect, the base layer needs to be tight, with its entire surface area in contact with your skin. There should be no loose material that may bunch up under your bibs and cause chafing, but also, it shouldn't be so tight as to restrict your movement or breathing.

OVERSHOES

These are a saviour on those frosty cold or wet days. They are not going to keep your feet dry in a torrential downpour but go a long way to keeping the cold out and your feet dry for longer. Usually made of breathable neoprene, they go over your road shoes, leaving your cleats exposed, and fasten at the back with a zip and/or Velcro.

ARM AND LEG WARMERS

Arm and leg/knee warmers are great because they are compact and easily removable. They have rubber grippers at the top that can be inserted under the sleeves of your jersey or the legs of your bib shorts, creating long sleeves/leggings, which can be easily removed if the weather improves. These are mainly used in spring and autumn when the day starts off cold but later warms up. Don't leave any skin showing between your arm warmers and your sleeves or your leg warmers and your shorts. And certainly no arm warmers with a sleeveless jersey.

SHAVING

Shaving your legs is a matter of personal preference. But if you do shave, make sure you do it regularly and get a smooth finish. Contrary to common belief, your everyday cyclist doesn't shave to make their legs more aerodynamic. The main reasons for shaving are ease of cleansing road rash, better pre- and post-race massages, and mostly importantly, because it looks good. Hairless legs show off muscle definition and look pro. There is a ritual aspect to it as well. I shave my legs for my first ride in bib shorts. Winter is over, the legs are out and the hair comes off. Joy.

THE DESIGNER'S VIEW
GRAEME RAEBURN,
CYCLEWEAR DESIGNER FOR RAPHA

Cycling has always been part of my life. I grew up in Kent in the middle of nowhere, and from a very young age, if I wanted to go anywhere, my bike was my ticket to freedom. I then studied fashion design, and freelanced alternately as a bike mechanic and a fashion designer. When I found (high end cyclewear brand) Rapha it was a stroke of luck really, that I could combine my two passions.

Probably the most important aspect of cyclewear is the fabric. Up until the '70s, wool was the fabric of choice, with its natural anti-microbial and temperature regulating qualities. These days you can get fabric to do pretty much anything, but the basic requirements are the same as they ever were; it needs to be lightweight, durable and snag-resistant. It needs to wick sweat away from the skin and to be anti-bacterial and non-odour absorbent. We need to be able to dye it in bright colours so that it can carry sponsors' logos, but it needs to stay colourfast. And of course, it needs to be comfortable. Once the fabric has been made and dyed, we add fabric 'finishes' to improve technical performance. These might include anti-microbial or bacterio-static or even insect repellent. And finally the fabric is made into the garment.

Rapha is now the designer for the Sky team – which has been a great experience. The riders are wearing their clothes to the max, and they'll often give us very blunt responses to garments, which we can then feed back into our mainline designs. So, for example, we noticed that some riders were chopping off the arms of their rain jackets just below the elbow so that they were cooler and easier to put on. We've now added a taped seam to our raincapes so that if you want to cut the sleeves, the fabric won't fray or be too baggy. When you talk to riders about a new product, they'll often respond in numbers. How much water a fabric absorbs leads to x amount of extra weight, which puts on y seconds to each hour of cycling. It's pretty fascinating. But ultimately you know you've designed a product well when there's no feedback. When a product is working, you don't even think about it.

Sponsorship is a key consideration as well. Back in the day, there was no sponsorship on National Champs jerseys. The jerseys were sacred, not to be defaced by advertising. There was the famous incident when Bernard Hinault was asked by his sponsors not to win the French National Championship so that they could keep their logo on his jersey. Recently there has been a bit of a backlash against sponsorship logos. In 2012, when the French National champ Nacer Bouhanni was riding for Française des Jeux, team manager Marc Madiot banned all logos from the French national champion's jersey, so sponsorship was only featured on their shorts. It looked pretty great actually.

My top tip for people interested in cycling fashion is to observe the pros. If you are really immersed in the world, you'll start to notice the emerging trends.

BIKE FIT

The late Marco Pantani, one of only seven riders to win both the Tour de France and Giro d'Italia in the same year, was renowned for his obsessive attention to detail. Pantani's bicycle sponsor manufactured 30 frames for him in one season alone. Angles were tweaked and tube lengths adjusted to suit the changing demands of the exacting Italian. Whilst this is probably excessive for most cyclists, it's crucial to get the fit of your bike right so that you can make the most of your riding potential. There are two fundamentals when establishing the correct bike fit for yourself; you have to be comfortable and the bike has to look good and therefore be in proportion.

It used to be that you straddled the top tube of the bike, and as long as it didn't cause damage to your nether regions, it was considered a fit. These days bike set up and fitting is a more complex and nuanced affair, best done by a trained fitter. If, however, you are doing it yourself, and/or you want to ensure the fitter is doing their job properly, there are a few basic guidelines that will help you get it right.

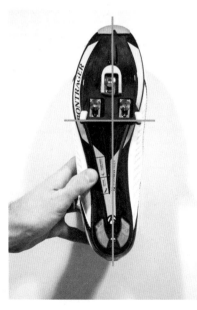

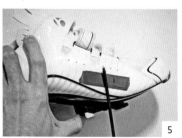

SETTING UP YOUR CLEATS

Before you begin a bike fit you will need to have your cycling shoes and cleats set up correctly. Pedals are the first point of contact with your bike and it is important to establish a neutral cleat position for a comfortable ride, and also to minimise your risk of injury.

- Put your shoes on without the cleats attached and do them up firmly. Stand with your weight evenly distributed between both feet (fig 1).
- Find a friend. Ask them to locate the bony protrusion at the base of your big toe (your first metatarsal head), and mark it with a piece of tape on the shoe. Do this on both shoes (fig 2).
- Take your shoe off and place the cleat on the bottom of the shoe. Leave it loose so you can move it about. Put your ruler on the mark and measure 10mm back, towards the heel. Make another mark at this point (fig 3).
- Find the centre of the cleat (sometimes indicated with a small notch), and line the centre up with the new mark (figs 4,5).
- Tighten the cleat, setting it horizontally so that it runs central from the heel and toe (fig 6).
- Any rotation of the cleat should be avoided. The pedal will allow for a degree of natural left and right foot movement through what's known as 'pedal float'.

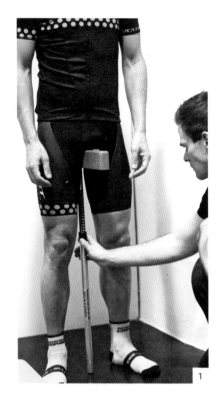

To establish what frame size you need, start by measuring your inseam as follows: Standing against a wall in bare feet, take a hardcover book, slide it up into the crotch, and mark the wall with a pencil (fig 1). Measure the distance from the floor to the mark for the inseam measurement. To find your frame size, take your inseam measurement and multiply it by 0.657. If my inseam measurement was 850mm, 850 x 0.657 = 558.45. From this I would be looking at a frame size of 55 or 56 centimetres.

Once you have your bike, you then need to adjust the contact points. Set it up on a turbo trainer, so that it is in a fixed position. Raise the front wheel slightly, so that the bike is level, and double check by running a spirit level across both front and back axles.

To establish saddle height, go back to your inseam measurement, and subtract 100mm – in my case this would be 750mm. Then measure that length from the centre of your bottom bracket along the seat tube to the top of the saddle to find the correct height (fig 2).

Ensure that your saddle is level and then set the height (fig 3). When you sit in the saddle, with your leg fully extended and your foot on the pedal, you should have a soft bend in your knee (fig 4). It should not be not be locked out straight. Also, as you pedal, your hips should not be rocking from side to side on the saddle.

To set your forwards or backwards position (fore/aft) on the saddle, a rough guide is that your knee should be directly over your pedal spindle. With your cranks level, a plumb line from the front of your knee should line up with your pedal spindle (fig 5).

SITTING PRETTY

The search for the ideal saddle can be difficult and often expensive – as really you need to buy different models to test them on the road. Contrary to popular belief, the softness of padding is not a key factor in comfort. In fact, a harder profile saddle offers better pelvic support and clearer feedback to the brain, allowing the rider to understand more about where they are positioned on the saddle. Saddle shape, width and profile are all matters of personal preference, but the most important thing is saddle position.

Ideal saddle set up is one that allows the rider to sit in the centre of the saddle with equal pressure on the sit bones on both sides. The sit bones should be supported by the widest part of the saddle and there should be little or no pressure on the soft tissue through the centre of pelvis. Saddle discomfort, sores and pins and needles or numbness are not normal and can be reduced by adjusting saddle position – sometimes even just by a few millimetres. A proper fitter might use pressure mapping technology to visualise the interface between the pelvis and the saddle. The maps below show two scenarios – in the one on the left, the weight is unevenly distributed. On the right it's even.

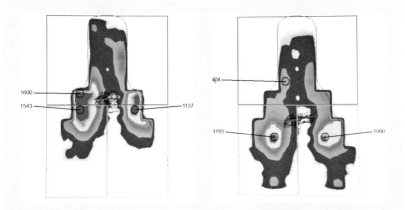

Establishing your reach is probably one of the most important factors when buying a bike. If you buy a bike with a reach that is too long, there is not much you can do to adjust it. If the reach is too short, you can extend it to some degree with different length stems.

As a rough guide, when you sit with your hands on the brake hoods, the angle between your back and your pelvis should be about 45 degrees, and the angle between your arms and your back should be about 90 degrees (fig 1). When on the hoods, you should have a soft bend in your elbow and not straight arms. It should feel natural, and you should be able to easily reach the brakes. If it is uncomfortable to ride with your hands on the brake hoods, the reach should be reduced.

For new riders, the handlebars should be no lower than six centimetres below the saddle (fig 2). If your flexibility is not great (ie. you struggle to touch your toes with straight legs), you may also need to raise the bars a bit to feel comfortable and eliminate tension in the neck and shoulders. This can be done by adding spacers under the stem depending how much room you have on the steerer. Make sure your bars are in a straight line with your stem – not angled up or down.

The width of your handlebars should correlate to the width of your shoulders. Measure across the front of your shoulders. The corresponding handlebar measurement is taken from centre of the right handlebar to the centre of the left handlebar (fig 3).

FRAME GEOMETRY

To really maximise your potential as a rider, it's definitely worth getting fitted up by a qualified bike fitter. After all, each body is different, and your bike needs to compliment the specifics of your dimensions and requirements. Frame geometry plays a key role in achieving perfect bike set up and riding position nirvana.

The contact points of a bike; handlebars, saddle and pedals (as determined by crank length and bottom bracket position), have a 'sweet spot' within their range of adjustment. This is the optimal positioning that fully maximises the potential of the frame, allowing you to get the best possible performance out of your bike. This sweet spot is largely determined by the frame's geometry.

However, as well as meeting the sweet spot, the ideal frame geometry has to also meet the various competing demands of the cyclist. It has to facilitate a sustainable, relaxed position on the flat, and aerodynamic positions on break-neck descents. It needs to handle predictably but also respond quickly to sudden manouevres around unexpected obstacles.

A skilled bike fitter will assess the rider's body dimensions, range of motion and flexibility, as well as their cycling aspirations, and then choose a frame that locates these contact points as close to the sweet spot as possible. They may try out different frame geometry options, or, even better, they may use an adjustable fitting 'jig', that allows them to assess contact point positions before trying out real bike frames.

If the frame geometry is wrong, then even a good set up (with the pedals, saddle height and reach in the correct position relative to each other) will not look right. For a bike to be in proper proportion, a reasonable length of seat post should be visible above the seat tube, the saddle should be positioned on the seat post around the centre of its rails and there should be a maximum of three centimetres of spacers (no spacers for the true aesthetes) placed beneath a moderate length of stem. Ideally, an angled stem should be positioned to point down. A bike with bad proportions will have a short stem pointing up with too many spacers, or a saddle mounted all the way forwards or backwards on its rails. This will not only look wrong, but will compromise the bike's handling.

In order to guarantee made-to-measure fit perfection, some riders choose to have a frame custom built for them. If this is not an option, there are plenty of good off-the-peg alternatives. These days, many manufacturers recognise that offering a range of frame geometries, rather than simply providing a selection of frame sizes, can better meet the requirements of a broader range of cyclists. The geometry options offered on stock bikes can be grouped into three broad categories:

> **'Pro' road geometry:** These frames feature longer top tubes and shorter head tubes to facilitate the long, low, aerodynamic positions favoured by many professional racers. This is great for aggressive riders and cyclists in good shape, who aim to ride regularly at high intensity. If, however, you have any issues with flexibility or core strength, this is going to be a very uncomfortable option, resulting in reduced performance and a lot of pain.
>
> **'Standard' road geometry:** These frames offer a moderate geometry that strikes a balance between aerodynamics and comfort, nimble handling and stability. Standard geometry is suitable for riders with good levels of flexibility and core strength who are looking for a bike that will work well for some intense riding as well as more leisurely sportives and randonees.
>
> **'Endurance' road geometry:** These frames often feature longer head tubes and shorter top tubes, offering a slightly more upright riding position and sometimes integrating vibration dampening design features. They are designed to deliver performance whilst also offering comfort and stability for long days in the saddle. Ideally suited to less flexible riders, but also to cyclists aiming for long-distance rides and sportive events.

In the table to the right, you can find definitions for some of the terms used to describe frame geometry as well as summaries of their influence on position and bike handling.

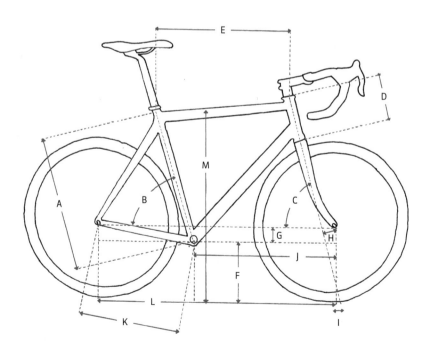

GEOMETRY TERM	MEASURED BY	INFLUENCES	TYPICAL RANGES
Seat tube length (A)	BB centre to top tube/seat tube intersection	- Proper seat height - Seat to handlebar relationship - Stand-over height	Relative to published frame size. A 56cm frame often features a 56cm seat tube
Seat tube angle (B)	Angle, measured clockwise from horizontal	Proper fore/aft position for power-weight distribution	71-75 degrees
Head tube angle (C)	Angle, measured clockwise from horizontal	- Weight distribution - Stability - Steering quickness - Head tube angle in combination with 'fork rake' establishes 'trail'	71-75 degrees
Head tube length (D)	Length, measured from bottom to top of head tube	- Range of adjustability or handlebar height. - Factor in position and weight distribution	Varies according to frame size but based on a 56cm frame it might be between 14cm (pro) to 17.5cm (endurance)
Effective top tube (E)	Length, measured horizontally	- Weight distribution - Reach - Choice of stem length to achieve handlebar position	Relative and often proportional to seat tube. A shorter top tube relative to seat tube generally results in a shorter reach
Bottom bracket height (F)	Ground to BB centre, adjusted for wheel size	- Centre of gravity - Handling - Cornering clearance (also influenced by crank length)	See 'bottom bracket drop'
Bottom bracket drop (G)	Vertical distance from wheel crank centre to BB centre	Related to BB height	7-8cm
Fork rake/offset (H)	Distance from front axle centre to line perpendicular to head tube axis	A longer rake means slower, more stable handling	40-50+mm
Trail (I)	Distance on ground between steering axis and front wheel contact	Like a shopping trolley trailing its wheels, trail influences the bike's capacity to self-centre	5.9-6.2cm
Front centre (J)	BB centre to front axle	- Handling via weight distribution - Determinant of wheel overlap	Varies with frame size
Chainstay length (K)	BB centre to R axle centre along stay	Handling via weight distribution and wheelbase	- Road 40-42cm - Cross 42.5-45cm - Track >38cm
Wheelbase (L)	Affected by head and seat tube angles, fork rake, top tube length and chainstay length	Longitudinal stability of a bike	97-101cm
Stand-over height (M)	Height of top tube relative to inseam of rider	Ability to stand over the top tube without hitting one's nether regions	Ranges from 1.5cm (road) to 10cm (MTB)

RIDING IN A GROUP

Riding in a group is what road cycling is all about. Drafting – the art of following the wheel in front, and thus sheltering yourself from the wind, allowing you to coast along effortlessly – is an experience completely unlike cycling solo. Regardless of whether or not you want to race, group riding is excellent practice. It will improve your bike handling skills, and increase your training benefit by allowing you to ride much faster and for far longer stretches than you could on your own.

Group riding requires a very specific set of skills, in order that you work effectively as part of the group. Once mastered, hand signals, drafting and safe conduct in a paceline will enhance the enjoyment of your ride as well as that of the people around you. But the most important thing to do is to observe and to be aware at all times of the other riders and the specifics of your environment.

If you are starting out, it's best to hang back and give yourself enough space to safely follow the wheel in front, holding your line without wandering around the road. Even if you are a strong rider, listen and take advice, and behave respectfully towards more experienced riders. If you are cocky and erratic, you will soon find yourself alienated. A good group will always accommodate any skill level, as long as the less experienced rider is willing to listen.

DRAFTING

Drafting is the technique whereby cyclists follow each other closely in order to benefit from the shelter that the person in front provides. As cyclists push through the air, they create a pocket of low pressure, known as 'slipstream', directly behind them, and an area of wind around them. By entering into the slipstream, you reduce the effort required to push forward, and also benefit from the eddies of wind around you, which propel you faster. Depending on the size of the group, you can save around 30 per cent of your energy through drafting. This percentage increases with more riders and other factors such as a bigger rider in front of you. Interestingly, even the person at the front of the group benefits from drafting, as the air that would normally drag back behind them is broken, improving their performance by about five per cent. Although, of course, they still have to ride hardest, and therefore each member of the group will take turns at the front.

The closer you get to the rider in front of you, the greater the benefit, so it's worth learning to hug that wheel. The pros keep a mere couple of centimetres between their wheel and that of the next rider. However, this can be daunting to begin with, especially if most of your training happens alone. Confidence will come from experience, and in the meantime, don't feel bad if you keep some length between the wheels. You will still feel a significant benefit even if you are a bike-length behind. The most important thing is not to place yourself or your fellow rider in any danger, so start with a distance that suits your skill level and then slowly bring it down as your bike-handling improves.

A good way to start is by practicing with one or two other riders. Try moving a foot or two laterally gently, getting a sense of where you get the most benefit (this will vary depending on the wind).

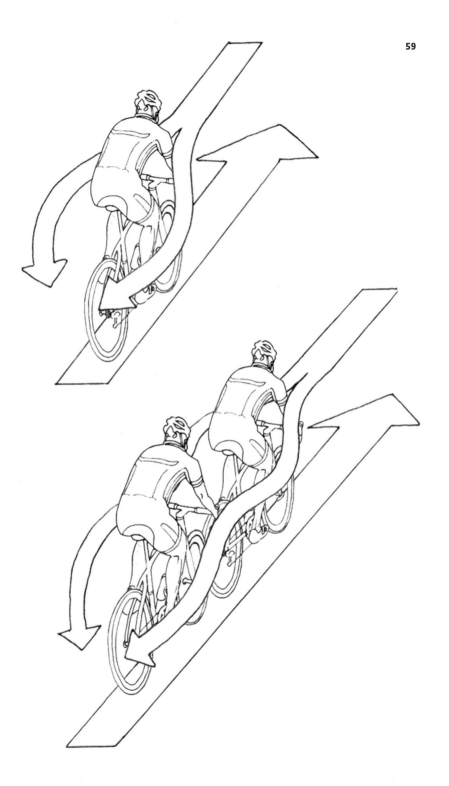

- The rider behind you needs to have confidence in you, so make all your moves obvious and predictable. Don't be erratic.
- Hold your line and don't deviate.
- No sharp movements left or right unless you are sure you have room.
- No sudden braking. Ride on the hoods of your brakes so you can feather them to slow down gently or to monitor your speed. Braking hard is a cardinal sin when riding in a group and may well result in a number of irate cyclists slammed up your backside. If it's an emergency, and sudden braking is essential, try to steer out of the group to avoid a pile up.
- Be aware of the people around you and warn others if they are being erratic. Take the advice if it is you that is being warned. You don't want to be that guy in the group.
- Don't stop pedalling. Maintain your pace in the group. Your cadence (pedal rate) shouldn't vary by much. Beginners often use too low a cadence, making the bike surge forward with each stroke. 80-90 revolutions per minute (rpm) is usually optimal. Practice pedal technique on your own until you can achieve a steady pace.
- When getting up out of the saddle your bike will surge backwards slightly – not good for the person following your wheel. Increase your pace as you get up out of the saddle to create more space between you and the rider behind, reducing the risk of touching wheels. Don't put your weight too far forward as you get up as this also causes a backwards lurch.
- The same goes when you sit back down from being up out of the saddle; your cadence should not change. If you stop pedalling, you will surge back into the person behind you.
- Always look ahead, not just at the wheel in front. You need to know where the road is going and how the group is moving.
- Anticipate gradients, choosing the right gear so that you can maintain your cadence.
- Communication is very important as visibility in the middle and back of the group is limited. People need to know what is coming up or what obstacles may be in the way. So it is important to use hand signals to indicate potential hazards like potholes, gravel, road furniture or even parked cars (see p. 63).

Hand signals are your main means of communication when riding in a group. Nobody wants their rim buckled from an unexpected pothole, a puncture from stray glass on the road or to hit a parked car, so each cyclist is relying on the person in front to indicate these potential hazards as well as communicate any turns or unexpected stops.

POTHOLE OR HAZARD

Potholes or hazards lying on the road like sticks or stones need to be pointed out. Simply indicating with a pointed finger in the direction of the hazard should be enough. Give this warning well before it is near you and move predictably away from the hazard, giving people behind you plenty of time to react.

GLASS OR LOOSE GRAVEL

The shake of a flat hand in the direction of the hazard indicates that there is loose gravel or glass on the road ahead.

Hazard left   Loose surface

Indicating with your arm behind your back or sometimes waving your arm behind your back, signals to move over as there is an obstacle ahead. Left arm indicates that you should move to the right, as there is an obstacle on the left, and vice versa for right. Sometimes you may need to wave riders into single file as the hazard ahead means there is not enough room for cyclists to ride two abreast. This may be oncoming traffic on a narrow road, or an increase in traffic as you approach a town.

SLOWING OR STOPPING

A hand held out, palm facing the rider behind indicates that you are stopping or just slowing. Mostly used when approaching traffic lights, intersections and roundabouts.

STOPPING FOR A MECHANICAL OR PUNCTURE

When you need to stop, to fix a puncture or a mechanical, put your arm up, hold your line and stop pedalling so that riders can safely pass you. Once they are all past, you can stop and repair the damage.

Move to right   Stopping mechanical   Stopping/slowing   Turning right

Hold your arm out and point to indicate the direction you are going to turn, and take a quick glance over your shoulder to make sure it's all clear. Do this with plenty of time to spare so everybody is able to react safely. This is good practice when riding solo as well so that cars and pedestrians are aware of your intentions.

VERBAL CALLS WITH THESE SIGNALS

Most minor hazards only need a hand gesture. Use verbal calls sparingly – there is nothing more annoying than a group of riders shouting out obvious obstacles every five minutes.

'Car up' means a vehicle advancing on a single track road, meaning you should form a single line, or just get in tighter to the side of the road. This is accompanied with a hand gesture to indicate what side the hazard is on.

'Car back' is shouted when a vehicle is behind and trying to overtake the group. Obviously there is no hand signal for this as it is the rider behind you that is calling out the hazard. Only use this if the driver cannot pass safely and riders need to be aware, like on a small lane or road.

'Riders up' this is called when passing other riders on the road. If you are in the UK / Australia you would indicate with your left arm and move to your right and vice versa in Europe / America.

'Slowing' or 'stopping' generally you would call out 'stopping' if you were coming up to a red light or 'slowing' if you are approaching a roundabout or some stationary traffic for example, accompanying this with the flat palm hand gesture.

'Turning left/right' make this call before you turn, accompanying it with the relevant gesture.

'**Clear'** is shouted when turning into a road where there is potential for oncoming traffic to indicate that it is safe to keep riding.

When you ride in a group you will, for the most part, be cycling two abreast wherever the road allows it. This makes the ride a more sociable experience and keeps the group together with no unaccounted-for stragglers. A good group will cater to all abilities with the stronger riders sitting on the front, and weaker riders towards the back. As the saying goes, you are only as fast as the slowest rider.

In this kind of general group ride, there will not be a lot of movement in positions. People will sit on the front for long periods, only changing if they need a rest or want a chat with another rider. When there is a change of position, the rider on the front will move forward and pull over to the side, allowing the person behind to pull alongside them, and rotating all the positions behind (see p.68).

ETIQUETTE FOR A GENERAL GROUP RIDE:

- Get as close to the person in front as you comfortably can – at the most a bike-length away. Ride close to the rider at your side as well, so you can further shield each other from air resistance.
- Never allow your wheel to cross over with that of the person in front. If they make a sudden sideways move and your wheels are overlapping, you will both almost certainly take a tumble.
- Don't ride three abreast on the road – it makes other riders nervous and drivers angry (we get enough grief from drivers for riding two abreast!). If you need to communicate something important to other riders, make it quick – don't stay there.
- Don't surge in the group. Hold your line – there is a time and a place for riding hard and it's not here. If you are feeling strong and the group is not going fast enough for you, have a turn on the front.
- Don't wander around the road. Tight lines are important, and you must be predictable both to your fellow riders and the traffic around you. It is especially important when descending in a group to maintain your formation. When riders overtake on descent it can cause confusion and put people in danger.

- Stay even with the rider next to you. 'Half-wheeling' is a cardinal sin. This is riding half a wheel length ahead of the person next to you. As the rider catches up, you pull ahead half a wheel again, causing a yo-yo effect. It is very annoying, disrupts the pace of the group and is a quick way to lose friends.
- When the road narrows or there is a lot of traffic, like when you enter a town, fall into single file.
- When stopping at traffic lights, don't leapfrog the other riders or bunch up in a group. When pulling away from the lights, do so in formation, not all over the road.
- Show respect for people around you and the environment. Don't clear your nose or spit while in line with others. If it's safe, pull to one side or go to the back of the group to do your gobbing. Don't litter either. Always take your empty gel wrappers, punctured inner tubes and other detritus with you. It's acceptable, and even encouraged to shout at any such offenders.

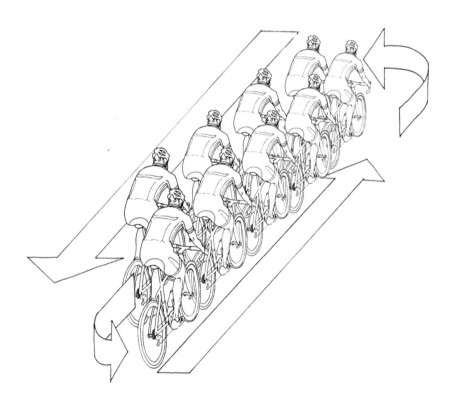

A single or standard paceline will normally be faster than a general group ride, and is probably the most common form of group riding. A small group of riders cycle in single file, with each person drafting as close as possible to the rider in front. There is a constant rotation of positions, with each rider taking a turn on the front, known as 'taking a pull'. This effort usually lasts for about 20-30 seconds, and when finished, the lead rider moves slightly to the left or right and drifts to the back of the line, allowing the rider behind to move to the front. When drifting back, don't switch off. When you are level with the last rider, start to accelerate, so you can easily get into their slipstream. If you leave your acceleration until they have past, you will find yourself wasting valuable energy to get back on.

If you are not feeling that strong, you can swing off the front earlier or even indicate you are not coming through and stay on the back – there is no shame in this. Likewise, if you are on good form you can stay up there longer. However, do not increase your pace. Pulling off the front will break up the group and cause fellow riders to burn up energy catching up. It is very common early in the ride, when your legs are fresh, to feel that you want to increase the pace, but in an hour or so things soon change, and a smooth, constant pace benefits everyone in the group.

THE WIND FACTOR

Something to bear in mind when riding in a single paceline is the direction of the wind, as this will affect where you position yourself in relation to the rider in front. If you are riding into a head or tailwind, position yourself directly behind the rider in front. If there is a crosswind, you need to position yourself slightly to the left or right of the rider in front, in order to maximise the shelter and in turn to increase your slipstream.

If the crosswind is coming from the left, position yourself slightly to the right of the rider in front. When swinging off, filter to the left, allowing the rider behind to come up on your right hand side, so that they advance in the lee of the wind. As you filter to the back, you will position yourself to the right of the rider at the back.

Reverse this if the wind is coming from the right; position yourself to the left of the rider in front. When your time is up on the front you will fall back on the right hand side, allowing the rider behind to come up on the left. Reposition yourself at the back slightly to the left of the rider at the end.

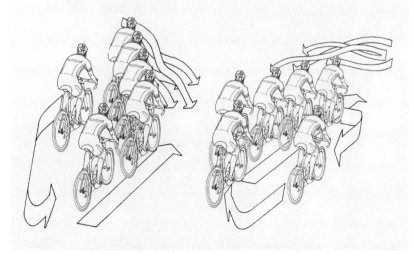

ROTATING PACELINE
(AKA 'THROUGH AND OFF' OR CHAINGANG)

A rotating paceline, also known as 'through and off', is a more intense ride – better for serious training or for cycling in a bigger group. Essentially, a rotating paceline is the same as a general group ride (see illustration on p. 68), except that the rotation is constant. You will come up on the outside line (the one closer to the centre of the road), and as soon as you get to the front, you will pull over to the line on the kerbside, and maintain your pace as the rider that was behind you moves in front of you. Effectively you have a constant anti-clockwise rotation, with the kerbside line seemingly moving backwards, and the traffic-side line moving forwards. In advanced group rides this movement may be reversed to move clockwise, depending on wind direction.

This method is much more efficient than a single paceline, because you are shielded from the wind while moving to the front as well as the back, meaning the whole group can go faster and further. The downside is that it's very intense – and demands full concentration with no time to chat or daydream. A good group will maintain a constant pace, creating a smooth, fluid, unified entity like a formation of starlings.

A FEW RULES OF THUMB IN A ROTATING PACELINE

- It is important to stay focused and follow the wheel in front, not allowing a gap that needs to filled by a sudden acceleration. This will only disrupt the group, causing a concertina effect and wasting energy.
- It is vital to maintain a constant pace. Don't surge forward when you get to the front as this will break the group up.
- Make all your movements obvious, no erratic moves to the left or right or grabbing handfuls of brake.
- Communicate to other riders. If you are tired, stay on the back, but let the rider in front know that you are not coming through and they can move forward in the line. You only have to do as much as you can.

Once you have mastered the basics of group riding, you may want to try your hand at riding a cyclosportive, or even road racing. However, mass start events can be intimidating, with many riders jostling for position in tightly packed groups. In the heat of the moment, etiquette and good riding practice can be quickly forgotten.

There are a few things to bear in mind so you don't end up at the bottom of a pile of twisted metal and snapped carbon.

IF IN DOUBT, ERR ON THE SIDE OF CAUTION

Watching the Tour de France, you'd be forgiven for thinking that at much lower speeds, an amateur race is a safer place to be. In fact, although crashes do occur in the Tour, the opposite is largely true; the more experienced the group, the fewer unnecessary risks are taken. Inexperienced riders can be nervous and erratic, clutching handfuls of brake or engaging in foolhardy manoeuvres, such as attacking up the wrong side of the road into oncoming traffic.

The consequences of having an accident on a road bike can be serious, and the risks are increased when riding in a group. The point is, err on the side of caution and don't feel pressured into stepping too far out of your comfort zone before you are ready. Focus on building up your bike handling skills in a quiet, traffic free environment, and don't take unnecessary risks. Some of the cardinal sins include, but are not limited to:

- Riding on the wrong side of the road into oncoming traffic (the worst offender).
- Cutting into the line of a fellow competitor in a corner.
- Resting your forearms on the flat part of the handlebar to gain an aerodynamic advantage (thus losing all ability to control your bike).
- Trying to do things you have seen in a race on television that are beyond your skill level (such as putting on a rain cape in the middle of the bunch, for example).

'Surging' is probably one of the most frequently occurring errors riders make when riding in a road race breakaway, or while sharing the effort in a sportive. Effectively this entails riders going too hard on the front, or accelerating too quickly as they move up the paceline. This creates gaps in the group, reduces efficiency, and eventually results in the group peaking too early and plunging, possibly irrevocably, into the 'red' zone.

In a race scenario, riding smoothly is all the more important because the effects of not doing so are amplified at higher speeds. Generally, an inexperienced group will try to ride too fast before they are familiar with the correct technique. Try and encourage your group (by asking nicely rather than shouting) to back off the pace a little, particularly on the climbs, and focus on working as a tight unit. You will almost certainly find that the group's average pace will increase.

DON'T DIE ON THE HILL

In the film *American Flyers*, Kevin Costner's rival, Barry 'The Cannibal' Muzzen famously tells his teammates not to pursue David Sommers when he attacks at the start of the race because 'he'll die on the hill!' Of course, Sommers goes on to claim a famous victory, but in reality this rarely happens. Using up your big efforts too early in an event will almost inevitably lead to early burnout, and you need to plan where you're going to spend your energy. Take the time to familiarise yourself with the course before you embark. If you know that 3,000 metres of climbing awaits you during the event, it probably isn't a great idea to attack early. Similarly, if there is a lengthy flat section before the first hill, don't plug away on the front in the wind. Instead, take full advantage of the drafting effects, leaving you fresher for the finale. None of this means you should be lazy, but be smart. Remember, there are no prizes for working the hardest!

THE PRO'S VIEW
DAVID SMITH,
EX-ROAD RACER FOR TEAM DFL AND
VC LYON VAULX-EN-VÉLIN

Road racing is about more than just being the fittest and being able to produce the most watts. The concentration and nerve required to remain in the first 20 riders is phenomenal. You have to constantly anticipate the next wave of accelerations, as everybody attempts to follow the rider who is attacking. If you get stuck on the wheel of someone who fails to react quickly enough, you can lose 40 or 50 places before you know what has hit you.

I vividly remember the point at which I realised that I perhaps didn't have what it took to compete in professional racing. The race was Paris-Connerré, a 175km blast across the plains to the west of the French capital. As we rode to the *départ réel*, I could sense the panic. Everybody knew we would be racing in a strong crosswind, and the moment the hammer went down, the crosswinds would force the peloton into a long line in the gutter, eventually splitting the bunch into several groups. Those at the back would effectively be out of the race.

A race official stood on the grassy verge attempting to prevent anyone from inching past him before he dropped the flag. It was total pandemonium. The guys near the back were dismounting their bikes, vaulting the roadside ditch and running through the adjacent field in an effort to get closer to the front. The race official eventually gave up and jumped in the lead car. As he did so, 200 cyclists accelerated as hard as possible, and the race was on.

I knew I should have taken to the field as well. But in the mayhem I stood calmly where I was, wondering what I was doing in a bleak, windswept field, risking life and limb for the chance to win an event few people had ever even heard of. Hence – unsurprisingly – I was near the back. The road was narrow, and within half a kilometre, I got stopped behind the first pile-up. Although the race was long, I was on the back foot already.

Once past the tangle of bikes and bodies, I managed to join a group that was working well together. We took turns in sharing the pace, riding as hard as we could to try and regain ground. As we began to tire, gaps would open up, jeopardising our efficiency. Tempers began to fray in desperation, and certain members of the group would unleash the occasional diatribe on those they felt weren't contributing sufficiently.

After a long chase we nevertheless made it back into the main group, but the damage was done. The energy I had expended in the violent pursuit meant I was unable to fight for position in the group as well as I needed to. My reactions to the ensuing accelerations were sluggish, and I repeatedly slipped towards the back of the bunch. After around 80km, the group split definitively in the relentless buffeting of the crosswind. In the company of a couple of other stragglers, I was left to watch the race slowly pull away as I tried in vain to close the gap. It wasn't only the race leaders that disappeared up that long, straight road on that autumnal day in northern France. So too did my aspirations of becoming a superstar of the professional cycling world. But it wasn't all time wasted. I've found my experience of racing in large groups has prepared me very well for another of cycling's many tribulations; the madness that is the London cycle commute.

TECHNIQUE

If you've ever ridden behind a good road cyclist, you'll understand the importance of technique. The pedalling, gearing and braking are all so smooth and fluid as to be imperceptible. The hips are still, the cadence steady as a heartbeat. They are one with the bike. No piece of expensive kit is going to get you to that place. The only thing you can do is observe how others do it and practice, practice, practice.

Technique is often a factor of fitness. Climbing technique, for example, which is not covered in this chapter, is pretty much a direct function of how fit you are, and how steady you can keep your cadence on the ascent. Descending, on the other hand, is all about bike-handling, and requires quite complex techniques in order to master it to its best (and most enjoyable) effect. Pedalling, gearing and braking require a combination of experience and common sense.

Watch the pros in their races, and listen to the more experienced members of your group. The more you embed the movement patterns of good technique into your neuromuscular pathways, the closer you're going to get to that effortless glide.

Pedalling technique is a much debated issue, with many cycling gurus advocating the concept of 'using the whole of the pedal stroke' by pulling on the upwards stroke as well as pushing on the downwards. I'm not a great believer in this philosophy. The best literature on this, in my opinion, comes from Dr Jeff Broker, who has dedicated over a decade of research to the art of pedalling.

According to Dr Broker, pulling up on the pedal does not increase maximal power output, and in fact it can cause injury. Pulling the pedal up puts a lot of pressure on the hamstrings and the hip flexors. These muscles are designed to lift the weight of the leg against gravity whilst running or walking and struggle to cope with the demand of contracting repeatedly against the resistance of the pedal. As the muscle fatigues, this increases tightness, which can contribute to lower back and hip pain. In addition to this, at recommended cadences of 80-90rpm, the muscular system cannot contract and relax quick enough to deactivate one group of muscles and contract another. In other words, as the left leg pushes down, the right leg cannot get out of the way quick enough to create negative pressure on the pedal, let alone generate force in an upwards direction.

In short, pulling on the upstroke does not work. So what is the correct pedal technique? Dr Broker advocates directing all your power into the downward stroke, starting the stroke at 12 o'clock, and ending it at 6 o'clock. This is termed the 'drive phase'. As the drive phase is coming to an end on one leg, it should be beginning on the other leg, while the first leg relaxes. Peak torque during the drive phase should occur around the 3 o'clock position.

SOME PEDALLING EXERCISES

- If you have gotten used to 'push/pull' pedalling, retrain your muscles to switch off on the upstroke by replacing your clipless pedals with flat pedals and doing some sessions with your bike on the turbo trainer.
- Note your average cadence on a normal, steady-state turbo session. Next time, try to increase it by 10rpm.

- This one-hour training session will focus your attention on pedalling: Warm up for 10 minutes. Every five minutes after that, shift your gears to the small ring and a big sprocket, and sprint as fast as you can for 10 seconds. Do this for 40 minutes, and then cool down for 10.
- 30-30s: Ride for 30 seconds at a super high cadence in a low gear, followed by 30 seconds of easy pedalling. Repeat this 10 times and do four sets, recovering for 10 minutes between sets.
- Muscle tension intervals: Pedal at 50-60rpm in a gear that keeps your heart rate below zone 3 (see p. 122). Focus on pushing down on the pedals, concentrating on the contractions of your gluteals, hamstrings and calves. Do this for 10-minute blocks, making sure your posture is correct and that your heel does not drop down.

■ Gluteals
▨ Quadriceps
■ Hamstrings
■ Calves

A common mistake of new cyclists is inefficient use of their gears. When moving from one gradient to another, it's crucial to shift gears swiftly so as not to lose momentum and precious energy. A good way of thinking about gears is that they are the means of keeping your cadence (pedalling rate) steady at 80-90rpm over a long period of time and a variety of gradients. Too high a cadence will lessen force and elevate heart rate, whilst laborious, lower pedal frequency will increase power per revolution and burn through fuel stores more swiftly. Switching gears nice and early will keep your pedalling more consistent, making your ride smooth and fluid.

Most bike set ups these days come equipped with what is known as a compact chain set as standard: A 50-tooth outer front chainring / 32-tooth inner front chainring coupled with a rear cassette ranging from 11 up to 32 tooth sprockets in varying ranges (12/23, 12/27, 11/28 etc). Try to avoid using the opposing extremes on your chain and cassette. You don't want to be in the big chainring on the front and the big sprocket on the back or the small chainring on the front and small sprocket at the back. This will result in a less than optimal chain line that will increase stress and rate of wear on your chain, front chainrings and rear cassette.

Most chain drops result from changing up and down from the small chainring to the large chainring on the front whilst under continued load. It's best to ease off pressure for a split second to allow the change to occur more freely, similarly to the way you engage the clutch in a car before changing gears. Start by moving the chain towards the centre of the rear cassette a couple of clicks, and then move the front chainrings up or down. This will lessen the chance of dropping or jamming the chain.

The key to efficient gear use is anticipation. If you know what's ahead, whether it's a climb, a descent, a wet surface or an obstacle, you can have your gearing prepared. If you're on a descent and you can see a climb approaching, for example, change down on the rear cassette so that the chain is towards the middle of the block as you approach the climb. Then, as soon as you hit the climb you can change down easily on the front chainring. If you change under load (ie. once the gradient has increased) you will have lost all your momentum, forcing you to work harder as you crunch through the gears.

One of the best pieces of advice I was given when I started out, was not to be scared to get on the drops when going downhill. Basically, the lower your centre of gravity is, the more control you have over the bike (and the faster you go). Like anything else on the bike, this is a skill that needs to be learned and practiced, with confidence being a massive factor. I have ridden with people who effortlessly drop like a stone down the mountain, the gap between me and them growing with every corner. I am by no means a great descender, however, it is a magical sensation when you are racing downhill, getting the right line into the corners to make your descent smooth and fluid.

It's helpful to distinguish between straight line descending and the more complex art of cornering when discussing descent techniques:

STRAIGHT LINE DESCENDING

- Get on the drops. This lowers your centre of gravity, gives you greater control and also makes you more aerodynamic.
- Always look ahead. This sounds obvious, but things come up a lot quicker when descending, so stay alert.
- Keep a relaxed grip on the bars. Tensing up will make your bike handling less efficient. Remember to breathe, drop your shoulders, bend your elbows and try to keep it loose.
- Sit slightly off the saddle. This will give you a natural form of suspension, allowing you to respond to undulations in the road without bouncing around.
- Keep your legs turning over if you can. As well as keeping you fluid with the bike, this will stop your heart rate from coming down too much, and will also keep your legs warm.
- It is important to keep your upper body warm as well. Your chest is getting the full brunt of the wind on the descent, so dress appropriately.
- It takes longer to react when tearing down a mountain, so keep a good buffer between you and the rider in front.

Cornering is the key factor when it comes to descending. Do this well and it feels fantastic. Get it wrong and you risk crashing, leaving a lot of skin on the road. Unsurprisingly, it takes a bit of experience to build up confidence, and it's normal to feel nervous at first. The key elements are body and bike positioning.

- Get on the drops with your fingers on the brakes. Again, this increases your traction and control, and also distributes your body weight more evenly between the front and rear tyres. Sitting up on the hoods will make you top heavy and less stable.
- Always look beyond the corner. If you focus on the obstacle coming up at speed, (ie. the bend), you will just freeze up. Focus on the exit – past the corner to where you want to go.
- Keep your body in line with your bike as much as possible. Lean into the corner with the bike, not just with your body.
- Keep your inside leg up and your outside leg straight, bearing the bulk of your weight. This will prevent your pedal touching the ground and potentially flipping you off the bike. With your weight on the outside leg, extend your inside arm slightly. This will distribute your body weight more evenly, giving you more traction on the road, keeping the bike rigid, and enabling you to cut a tighter line.
- You can also move back slightly on the saddle, shifting your weight away from the front.
- Stay light in the saddle so that you can respond better to the varying road surfaces and bumps.
- As you approach the corner, you need to swiftly assess the situation; how tight is it? Are there any hazards such as potholes or gravel? Are there oncoming cars or other riders? These things will determine how fast you can take the corner, and whether you can risk going onto the wrong side of the road.
- If conditions are wet, make sure you slow right down – your traction will be severely compromised. Also, keep an eagle eye out for manhole covers and road markings – these get very slippery when wet.

- Brake before you enter the corner. You want to wash off some speed before you hit the corner, not when you're already in it. Braking hard while cornering will severely compromise your traction on the road and could cause you to skid.
- If it is a tight hairpin bend, or you are unsure, slow right down and brake before the bend. If it's a softer, wider corner, you can hit it at speed.
- Once you've established the corner, set up your approach. Enter the corner as wide as possible, cutting in as close to its apex as you can, then exit as wide as you can on the opposite side – thus straightening the corner out as much as possible.

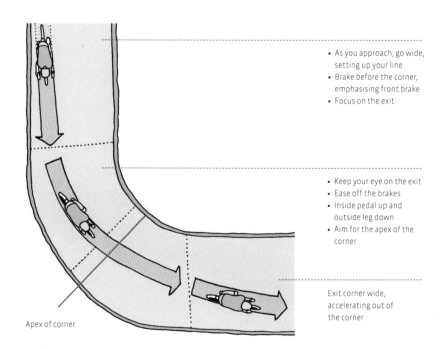

- As you approach, go wide, setting up your line
- Brake before the corner, emphasising front brake
- Focus on the exit

- Keep your eye on the exit
- Ease off the brakes
- Inside pedal up and outside leg down
- Aim for the apex of the corner

Exit corner wide, accelerating out of the corner

Apex of corner

Braking is a surprisingly complex skill that, as with all aspects of bike handling, only improves with practice. As you may have noticed, your bike has two brakes – one on the front wheel and one on the back. When braking, it's important to use both of them. The front brake is most effective at stopping you. A lot of newer cyclists shy away from putting too much front brake on, fearing they will go over the bars or the front wheel will slide out from under them. These scenarios can occur, but only if the front is deployed in the wrong situations. In normal, dry conditions, applying more front brake – or even solely front brake – will stop you faster and 99 per cent of the time will not result in a skid.

When traction is poor (eg. in wet conditions, when there is a lot of loose gravel on the road, or in the unusual circumstance of braking whilst cornering), the front brake is a riskier strategy, and may well end up in a skid. In these conditions, use the back brake to slow you down. Rather than grabbing handfuls of brake, increase the pressure slowly, giving yourself plenty of time to slow and stop. Practice braking hard, and then releasing the brake and reapplying it. This is a good strategy for a faster stop, as it can help you gain some control over your bike and prevent a skid situation – a little like the ABS brakes on a car.

SOME BRAKING TIPS

- When applying the front brake hard to stop as quickly as possible, lock your arms out in front of you to brace yourself against the deceleration.
- While braking, shift your weight as far back as you can comfortably go. By keeping your centre of gravity low and far back, you'll maximise your traction and minimise the risk of going head over handlebars.
- A good tip in the wet is to lightly apply your brakes so that the pads drag lightly on the wheels' rims. This will help clear excess water and improve the efficacy of the brakes.
- As a rule, feather your brakes to slow gradually. Especially in a group ride, avoid grabbing handfuls of brake.

Bunny hopping is the art of lifting both wheels off the ground at the same time, and is an essential skill to master if you are planning on riding in a group. When you are in a paceline, swerving left or right to avoid potholes, sticks or stones comes at the risk of taking out a fellow rider. Jumping over the obstacle and maintaining a straight line is the best way of avoiding hitting whatever is in your path.

Bunny hopping is a little bit easier with clipless pedals, but possible without as well:

- Start by placing a small object on the ground. Roll towards it, standing up out of the saddle. Try to clear it first with just your front wheel, pulling hard on the handlebars until it comes up. You're aiming to do this with maximum control, so the wheel doesn't slap back down.
- Do the same with the rear wheel, again out of the saddle, exploding your legs upward to lift it.
- Now you need to combine the two actions. Roll towards the object, lift the front wheel and immediately after, the back wheel to clear it completely.
- Once you have this down, add some speed and try to make the two actions simultaneous. Make sure you are out of the saddle, bend your arms and legs slightly, pull hard on the handlebars, and as your front wheel comes up, explode your legs upward, to lift the rear. Level out and land the bike in a controlled manner. It's a great feeling.

TRAINING

You may be able to get pretty fit by winging it, but to push your body, and your cycling ambitions, to higher levels, you have to get serious about your training. And you also have to get organised. Training schedules don't make themselves – especially when work and/or family demands leave little time in the week for riding.

Before you get stuck into the specifics of training plans, it's worth bearing in mind the F.I.T.T principles (yes it's an annoying acronym, but it does work!):

Frequency: Be realistic about how much time you have available and set aside slots in the week in which you can consistently train (for many riders this would be the weekend). Build in additional sessions and recovery days around them.

Intensity: Be honest with yourself about your strengths and weaknesses. Keeping a ride journal is a good place to begin. Following a ride or event, note down your sensations. When did you feel strong? What happened when you felt weak or got dropped? This will help you to determine which areas you need to improve and which intensity to focus on. A helpful principle is to plan your training days, when you have more time available, for longer, low-intensity rides and then slot in shorter, focussed, high-intensity rides, perhaps on a turbo trainer, as and when you can.

Time: Work out how many hours you have available per training session, and target your energy systems according to the length of session. Low intensity rides will be longer, whilst a high intensity training session can be fitted into 45 minutes. Don't be tempted to allot all of your available hours to cycling. Plan time for strength and conditioning training and stretching.

Type: Make sure your training is specific to your objectives, focusing on your weak areas, and is also varied so that your body (and more importantly, your mind), doesn't get stuck in a rut.

This chapter will outline some further guidelines to help you make the most of whatever time you have, with a little bit of physiology and fuelling info thrown in for good measure. But when training, the most important thing to do is enjoy it. After all, most of us are not getting paid for it!

ENERGY

Before you start planning your schedule, it's useful to have a clearer understanding of what it is that you're targeting with your training. We humans are complex animals, and our bodies are suited to lots of different activities from sprinting to endurance. These activities all require fuel in the form of energy, but different activities require different types of energy.

Adenosine Triphosphate, or ATP, is a high-energy molecule that serves as the basic currency for our energy levels. When ATP breaks down, energy is released. We need an awful lot of ATP to get through the day – but the store of ATP within our bodies' cells is very small. Therefore, we have to continually resynthesise ATP to provide us with energy. When people talk about 'energy metabolism' they are referring to the energy systems in our bodies that replenish ATP. There are three such systems, each of which contribute in different proportions depending on the duration and intensity of the effort. I will try to explain these systems in a nutshell.

Energy System 1 – ATP-PC: This is the reaction involving ATP and another high-energy molecule called phosphocreatine (PC). The ATP-PC reaction takes place in the absence of oxygen and can provide a lot of energy quickly, but only for very short periods of under 10 seconds. If you want to see a highly developed ATP-PC system in action, watch Mark Cavendish's burst in the final 200 metres before the finish line.

Energy System 2 – Anaerobic Glycolysis: The human body has around 2,000 calories of carbohydrate, stored in the tissues of the liver and muscles in the form of a chemical compound called glycogen (basically a type of starch). Without the presence of oxygen, this carbohydrate can be broken down in a chemical reaction called anaerobic glycolysis, which results in an inefficient, but speedy production of energy. Whilst only five per cent of the energy potential of a glucose molecule can be realised, the energy is liberated quickly – ideal for high intensity efforts that last between 10 seconds and two minutes. Anaerobic glycolysis creates lactate, the base of lactic acid.

Measuring blood lactate concentration is a useful way to gauge the intensity of a rider's effort.

Riders such as Philippe Gilbert use their anaerobic energy system to generate spectacular performances in the finales of races. The majority of the 1,300 metre climb of the Mur de Huy, the site of the finish line of the Flèche Wallonne, reaches a 26 per cent grade and required Philippe to produce an explosive 2:44 minute effort when he won the race in 2011.

Energy System 3 – Aerobic Metabolism: The term aerobic refers to the presence of oxygen in a process. When oxygen is introduced, the breakdown of glucose, fat and protein can be turned into energy in a much more efficient manner than without oxygen. This process takes a lot longer, and is therefore better over the longer stretches of lower intensity energy usage that make up most of your ride.

Fat can be a helpful factor in this process. The high-energy nature of fat molecules means that they can resynthesise even more ATP than glucose. A 75kg rider with 15 per cent body fat has 11.25kg of stored fat, representing 101,250 calories of energy potential. If the rider tried to use it all, they would die, but by developing their aerobic system through training, they will be able to ride at higher intensities using fat as their main fuel, thus preserving their stores of carbohydrate for the higher intensity efforts later in the ride.

For example, in Stage 18 of the 2013 Tour de France, Jens Voigt escaped in a breakaway group. The route covered 172.5km. According to his power meter, he recorded a 309 watt average power for the duration of the stage, expending over 1,000 calories per hour for over five hours, much of which would have been supplied by fat metabolism. Consequently, he had reserves of carbohydrate available to fuel the higher intensity efforts on the stage, such as when he averaged 390 watts on the climb of the Col de Manse.

It can be useful to think of these three energy systems as fuel tanks. Tank one is filled with phosphocreatine feeding the ATP-PC system, tank two is filled with glucose feeding the anaerobic glycolysis system, and tank three is filled with a cocktail of carbohydrate, protein and fat, feeding the aerobic metabolism. Our bodies draw on all three tanks regardless of the type of effort, but the systems contribute in different proportions depending on the duration and intensity of the effort.

You can improve the efficiency of each tank by focusing your training in different ways. Lots of long (90 minutes or more) low intensity rides will be beneficial to the aerobic system, and are a good place to start. This type of 'base training' will quickly bring to light what your strengths and weaknesses are, and from there you can take on more specific types of training to address the problem areas. A rider who struggles on long climbs, for example, may aim to develop their aerobic energy system at higher training intensities, whilst a rider who is always beaten in the town-sign sprint, might want to focus their training on their 10 second efforts fueled by their ATP-PC system.

Fuel tank/energy system	Fuel type	Best suited for	Example effort
ATP-PC system	Phosphocreatine	Efforts up to 10 seconds	Final 200m of a sprint
Anaerobic glycolysis	Glucose	Efforts less than 2min in duration	Riding hard up a short, steep hill
Aerobic system	Carbohydrate, fat, protein	Longer duration efforts	40km time trial, long alpine climb

You're now ready to build your training schedule. As mentioned in the intro to this chapter, you need to work out how much time you have in the week, and build up a schedule that has space for long, low-intensity rides, which target your aerobic system as well as shorter, high-intensity sessions that build up your anaerobic fuel tank. There are a few guiding principles to bear in mind before you draw up your schedule.

MAKE IT SPECIFIC

The training of many cyclists is simply too general. Hours of riding at 28km/h in fair weather will make you very good at riding at 28km/h. But as soon as you find yourself needing to change pace, or dealing with wet conditions or unusual circumstances, you might find you lack the capacity to face the challenge.

Long, steady rides are important to build an aerobic base, but you need to make sure your training is relevant to the type of cycling you intend to do. Decide on a specific event and prepare accordingly. If you are entering a sportive event, your training should focus on endurance and also tackle the various elements of the terrain; perhaps a long climb requiring you to maintain a high intensity for long periods; or cobbled sections, which call for some skill-based training. Look at the website of the event and check whether segments of a route exist on a website like Strava. Try to get a clear idea of what time and intensity of effort may be required to complete a particular section.

PROGRESSION AND OVERLOAD

The body is an incredible system. Providing it has sufficient time to recover, it will adapt to stresses so that it can tolerate them better next time they are encountered. Training should stress the body, and as the body grows stronger and adapts to the stimulus, the training should progress so that your rides become longer, more varied, or more intense than previously.

Training must force the body to work above its habitual level,
'overloading' it to stimulate adaptation. The question is how much to overload. Not training enough means that you fail to improve as much as you want. Training too much may leave your body exhausted and even injured. There is no easy answer – you need to develop a finely tuned sense of what's going on inside your body in order to make the right decisions about when to ride hard and when to back off. However, technology can help a bit. Heart rate monitors, power meters and lactate testing devices measure intensity of effort and provide a means to understand what is happening within the body,

TURBO TRAINERS VS. ROLLERS

Riding on the road is, of course, the most specific form of training. But only few live in areas with the variety of terrain, scarcity of traffic and temperate climate that allow them to rely on road training alone. For the rest of us, indoor training is a great option.

Both turbo trainers and rollers are useful for targeting specific energy systems and abilities. Rollers are the traditionalist's choice with the benefit that they stimulate the muscles in a similar way to riding on the road. They require the cyclist to balance and hold their riding line in a limited range, activating the stabilising muscles in a way that the turbo trainer doesn't. There is also an argument that they can help perfect one's pedal stroke – although the definition of 'perfect pedalling' is a much-debated issue. On the downside, most rollers don't create sufficient resistance to target the top-end training zones. Some newer models are beginning to address this issue, but most riders would choose a turbo trainer for specific interval training, as you can adjust the resistance levels and the cadence (pedalling speeds). You can also raise the front wheel of the bike with riser blocks (or a phone directory) to simulate the posture required on long climbs.

Ideally a rider would have access to both a roller and a turbo trainer, but if you have to choose one I would go with turbo for sheer versatility.

The concept of 'training zones' is useful to get a sense of how your body is responding to the pressures you are putting it under. A heart-rate monitor will help you work out your training zones, starting with zone 1, a very easy level of training which doesn't affect your heart rate much, and up to zone 6, which is basically full tilt – the hardest you can go. Time spent in this zone has to be done in short bursts, with a focus on speed and power.

By identifying what your zones are, you can plan your training sessions more intelligently, targeting specific energy systems.

DIY performance test: There are a number of different ways of establishing your training zones, but this is one of the simplest. On a turbo trainer, warm up for 20 minutes, then complete a 30-minute effort, cycling as hard as you can. Record your average heart rate for the final 20 minutes of this effort, using a heart rate monitor. Most devices will allow you to record data and then download and review it. If you don't have this option, you may need a friend to note down your heart rate every two minutes (or less) during the final 20 minutes, and then work out the average. Use this table to then calculate your zones:

Zone	Percentage of average heart rate (from 20 min test)	Perceived intensity	Accumulated time in zone during a training session targeting this zone	Example efforts
Zone 1	< 68% HR not to go above this %	Easy	1-3 hrs	1-3 hr recovery ride
Zone 2	69% - 83% HR to stay between these %	Steady	1-7 hrs	Long endurance ride at steady rate
Zone 3	84% - 94% HR to stay between these %	Comfortable	50-90 mins	Extended tempo efforts, perhaps for 1 hr in the middle of a 3 hr ride
Zone 4	95% - 105% HR to stay between these %	Uncomfortable	10-60 mins	3 x 10 min with 10 min recovery
Zone 5	>106% HR should be above this %	Hard	12-30 mins	3 min effort, with 3 min recovery, repeated 4 times
Zone 6	N/A	Very hard	10 sec - 2 mins.	30 sec maximal effort, 30 sec recovery, repeated

So, if for the 20 minutes of intensive riding, I had an average heart rate of 170bpm, then zone 1 would be 68 per cent of 170bpm = 116bpm, zone 2 is 69-83 per cent of 170bpm = 117-141bpm, etc.

Training at a moderate intensity all the time will lead to moderate fatigue, which will not stress any one energy system sufficiently. World class athletes' training records show that they spend a lot of time training in their 'easy' zones (1 and 2), and also in their 'very hard' zones (5 and 6), with little time spent in the middle. The benefit of spending a long time in zones 1 and 2 is that it develops the aerobic energy system without causing damage or long-term fatigue. Therefore, the body is ready for intense zone 5-6 efforts, which challenge the body by putting stress on all energy systems.

HIGH INTENSITY TRAINING (HIT)

In 2005, a study by Burgomaster et al. concluded that training at high intensity could be an effective alternative to long, time-consuming, low-intensity rides for improving endurance performance.

During the study, the subjects carried out a performance test, riding to exhaustion at 80 per cent of their peak power output. Following this, they carried out a 14-day experiment, in which they were required to make repeated 30 second efforts at well over 100 per cent of peak power, followed by four minute recovery times. This session was repeated three times a week over the 14 days. After this experiment, another performance test was conducted, and it was found that the participants in the programme had increased their time to exhaustion from 26 minutes to 51 minutes – a 96 per cent improvement!

Based on the Burgomaster study, HIT can substantially improve a rider's sustainable power output with just four to seven 30 second sprints with four minute recovery times between them, repeated three times a week.

Adaptation works both ways. Your body will respond to stimulus, but it will also respond to a lack of stimulus. In the absence of training, the body will begin to revert to its pre-training state. The key is to train consistently and sustainably, giving yourself time to recover, but not enough time for reversals. Older riders may find they need slightly more recovery time than younger riders. If this is the case, do not be afraid to take few days break between sessions, and listen even more carefully to your body. Do your legs feel heavy or painful? Is your heart rate taking a long time to increase? Try to distinguish between tiredness, which can be overcome through effort, and fatigue, which signals you need to rest. If it's clear that your body is not responding to your requests to ramp up the intensity, back off training for a couple days and then try again.

Boredom is the other big obstacle. Some cyclists will describe how their "head has fallen off", meaning they've lost their motivation. Tedium is often the result of too much of a particular type of training stimulus without sufficient recovery, leading to a state of psychological and/or physical fatigue. The antidote to tedious training is to combine training stimulus with sufficient recovery and vary the types of training you do.

LOSE WEIGHT OR GAIN POWER?

Cycling pundits are always raving about the exceptional 'power to weight' ratios of the world's top riders. And rightly so. Riders who can produce more power relative to their weight do not need to work as hard to reach the same speeds during accelerations, and the benefits are even more pronounced in climbs, where extra weight on steep gradients is a major disadvantage.

Training will help you to improve your performance through sustainable power-output, but there are also significant benefits to losing weight – either from your body or from your equipment. The excellent website *cyclingpowerlab.com* compares the benefits of losing weight vs. gaining power. The following example presents two scenarios based on a theoretical mountainous sportive event:

Scenario 1: Lose weight
Bike + rider weight = 93kg
Time to complete course = 6hrs, 03min, 25sec

Bike + rider weight = 88kg (minus 5kg)
Time to complete course = 5hrs, 51min, 44sec

Time saving = 11min, 41sec

Scenario 2: Improve sustainable power
Sustainable power = 244 watts
Time to complete course = 6hrs, 03min, 25sec

Sustainable power 264 watts = (8 per cent increase)
Time to complete course = 5hrs, 42min, 03sec

Time saving = 21min, 22sec

Ideally, the rider would lose weight and gain power, but the emphasis shifts depending on experience. An experienced rider may struggle to achieve large increases in sustainable power output and will be better off focusing on losing weight. A new rider can achieve big improvements in sustainable power and should invest their efforts in that area, as the impact will be much greater than weight loss.

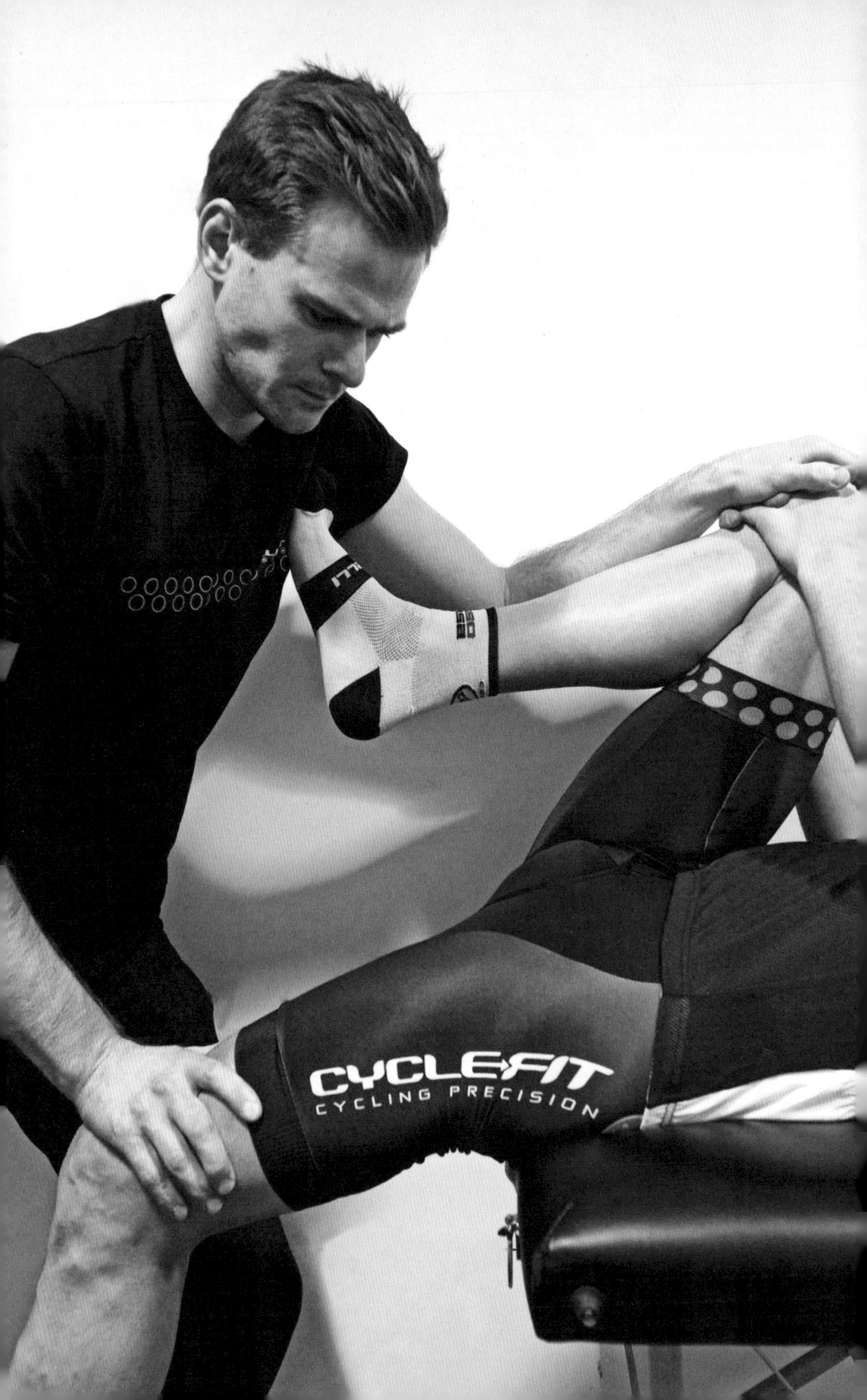
CYCLEFIT
CYCLING PRECISION

Training will help you build up your strength, but there is more than maximal power output to good physical conditioning. One of the major building blocks of cycling performance is mostability; core stability and a range of movement/flexibility. Although your legs are the most tangible source of power, without core muscles you have no foundation of movement for your pedalling and handling. By keeping your supporting muscles strong and your joints flexible, you can avoid the back pain, tight hip flexors and other niggles that bother even the strongest cyclist.

The following exercises will help you build up your mostability. The number of reps and the lengths of time stated here are meant as guides only – always start at a low level and build up. It goes without saying that if they result in any pain, stop them immediately.

■ Hip flexors
■ Gluteals
■ Quadriceps
■ Hamstrings
■ Calves
■ Tibialis anterior

Clamshell: Lie on one side, feet and knees together, with knees bent to 90 degrees. Keep your heels together and rotate the top knee out to the side as far as you can without rolling backwards at the pelvis. Aim for 20 slow, controlled reps. *Works: Gluteals.*

Single leg bridging: Lie on your back with knees and heels together and knees bent so that your feet lie flat on the floor. Take one foot off the floor and straighten the leg. Then, in a slow, controlled movement, pull in your core muscles to push through the other foot, lifting your bottom off the floor so that your body is straight and your spine is neutral. Hold the position at the top to increase the difficulty of the exercise and do 10 reps with 10 second holds for each leg. *Works: Gluteals.*

Single leg stand partial squat: Stand on one leg without holding onto anything. In a slow, controlled movement and without losing balance, allow your knee to bend until it's in line with the inside of the big toe. Aim for 20 reps on each leg. *Works: Gluteals and quads.*

Single leg sit to stand: Sit on a chair and take one foot off the floor. With your hands across your chest, lean forwards and stand without moving the foot. Return slowly to your sitting position without allowing your knees to roll inwards. Maintain good upright posture throughout. Aim for 20 reps on each leg. *Works: Gluteals and quads.*

Plank: Lie on your front, with your elbows supporting your upper body. Flex your feet so your toes are in contact with the floor and then lift your body up so that your spine is in a straight line. Aim to hold your position for 30 seconds and do three reps. As you get stronger, hold your position for longer. *Works: Core.*

Hamstring stretch: Place one foot flat on a low chair or bench in front of you with your knee slightly bent. Push your bottom out whilst leaning forward at the hips without flexing the spine. You should feel the stretch in the back of your upper leg. Progress by leaning further forward and attempting to push the bottom out harder. Hold for one minute and do three stretches for each leg.

Quad stretch: Standing on one leg, take hold of the ankle of the other leg and pull it in towards your bottom. Keep your knees together and hold onto a chair if you need support. Keep an upright posture and avoid arching your lower back by activating your core muscles. Hold for one minute and do three stretches for each leg.

Lunge hip flexor stretch: Stand with your feet together, then step forward with one leg into a lunge position. Bend the front leg so that the other leg is extended and your start to feel a stretch in the front of your hip and down the front of your upper leg. Hold for one minute and do three stretches for each leg.

Heel hang (calf stretch): Stand with the ball of one foot on the edge of a step. Allow the heel to slowly drop towards the floor. Regulate the stretch by taking some weight on the other leg. Hold for one minute and do three stretches for each leg.

It was once the wisdom of many (mainly French) cycling professionals, that the ideal preparation for a road race was a rare steak washed down with a glass of red wine. Up until the '70s, even the scientific community advised athletes to 'drink only a little water during exercise', and for many riders, drinking whilst racing was perceived as a sign of weakness.

These days, the science of fuelling and hydration is highly refined, with formulated gels, drinks and even post-ride intravenous drips on offer. Sports science is now so highly evolved that it can be confusing to an outsider. These are some guiding principles to help you through – although it's important to remember that each body is individual, and there will be an element of trial and error as you explore what brings out your best performance.

WHAT TO EAT BEFORE RIDING

Before rides under an hour: No special diet is required for short rides.
Before rides greater than an hour: If you're setting off on a relatively intense ride, it's a good idea to top up on carbohydrates. However, a pasta party and huge bowls of porridge on the day is probably overkill. Most riders consume enough carbs in their normal diet to ensure reasonable levels of stored carbohydrates, and you don't want to suffer gastric discomfort on your ride.

A good fuelling strategy is to top up carbohydrates two hours or more before you set off. Sweet potato, rice or oats are good options, alongside some easily digestible protein such as a whey protein powder. Try to avoid fats. And red wine. This is an example of a pre-sportive fuelling strategy:

- *Two hours before start:* Bowl of oats with scoop of whey protein (200 calories of carb and 20g protein)
- *Hour and a half before start:* Over 30 minutes, sip on a 500-750ml bottle of water mixed with 50g carb (200 calories of carb).
- *Hour before start:* Sip only plain water to avoid stimulating your body to secrete more insulin, resulting in a drop in blood sugar.

However, pre-ride meals should be a personal choice and, especially if you suffer from nerves, you might want to stick to an easy-to-digest liquid meal.

These days, it's quite common for pro-riders to share their power meter files from races and training, which gives a really interesting insight into how much energy a rider expends, and therefore how much they need to eat to make up for the effort.

In the 2013 Tour, Jens Voigt shared his power meter data from stage 18. Jens spent a lot of time driving the breakaway group during this stage, producing 5,800 kilojoules (kj) of energy over the course of 172.5km. The human body is only around 25 per cent efficient, so producing one kj requires the body to expend four kj. In other words, Voigt's body had to expend 23,200kj. There is approximately one calorie for every four kj, so we can estimate that the energy requirement for this stage was 5,800 calories. It took Jens Voigt five hours and 14 minutes to complete stage 18, meaning on average he was burning 1,105 calories per hour.

Most cyclists fuel themselves during rides with carbohydrate sources (CHO), as these are easier to absorb than proteins and fats. Most endurance athletes can only tolerate around 60-90g of CHO per hour (and for many it's much less). Each gram of CHO provides approximately four calories, meaning that for Jens to replenish the calories he was burning, he would have to consume 276g CHO per hour – obviously an impossibility.

What this illustrates is that it's often not possible, or even desirable, to consume the calories you are expending during your ride. This energy deficit is nothing to worry about. Most of the effort will be 'paid for' using the body's stored energy sources – primarily fat and glycogen (a form of stored carbohydrate). The deficit can be made up in the hours and days following the ride.

During rides under an hour: In exercise lasting less than one hour, consuming carbohydrate is generally not beneficial, unless you are undertaking repeated high intensity efforts, such as one-minute intervals with three-minute recoveries. In this case, carbohydrates may have a beneficial impact on the central nervous system.

During rides greater than an hour: For longer rides at intensities that will cause fatigue, consuming carbohydrate can be very helpful. The majority of riders can tolerate 30-60g of carbohydrate per hour – although this varies from person to person. These carbs can come from a range of sources including real food (bananas, figs and dates), or formulated products such as gels, bars and powders mixed with drinks. If you opt for the latter, you should aim for six to eight per cent carbohydrate concentration in the fluids, with lower concentrations on hot days. Products with multiple types of carbohydrates may be more easily absorbed into the body, but experiment. That's why there are so many products on the market – different combinations work for different bodies.

A basic indication of correct hydration is weight. You should drink enough to avoid losing too much weight, but not so much that you gain weight. Try a little experiment – weigh yourself before and after a ride, noting how much fluid you consumed en route. Most riders will tolerate losing two per cent of their body weight during a ride in cold to temperate conditions, but no more than that. Even a relatively low level of dehydration will be detrimental to performance, but if an athlete consumes more fluid than their sweat rate, they may be putting themselves at risk of hyponatraemia. As a general guideline, you should aim to consume 400-800ml per hour, with small amounts of sodium (0.3-0.7g per litre) and electrolytes added in if you so wish.

WHAT TO EAT AND DRINK AFTER RIDES

Following a long ride, you should aim to rehydrate and make up some of the energy you've lost. Consuming carbohydrates and protein immediately after the ride will help the recovery process. Research indicates that a 4:1 ratio of carbohydrate to protein may be beneficial. In terms of quantities, a rough guide of 0.8-1.5g carbohydrate per kg of body weight is a good starting point.

On the hydration front, you should be aiming to consume 150 per cent of the volume lost through sweating to return to a pre-exercise weight. For example, if a 70kg rider lost 1.4kg during an event, they may need to consume two litres of fluid to rehydrate. This should be drunk over the course of an hour or two, not all in one go.

SOME FUELLING POINTERS:

- Not all calories were created equal. A calorie consumed from a sugar source will have a different influence on the body than a calorie consumed from a fat source.
- Wherever possible, aim to meet your nutritional requirements with real food. However, where time is limited, it can be beneficial to stock up on processed products (protein powders, gels, bars etc).
- Achieving good body composition is not as simple as matching energy intake with expenditure; our bodies are not furnaces ready to burn up anything and everything, and you can't compensate for a poor diet with exercise.

THE SPORTS SCIENTIST'S VIEW
JAMES HEWITT,
CYCLING ANALYST FOR CYCLEFIT

Until 2005, I was an Elite Espoir (Under-23) racing cyclist based in the South of France, aiming to secure a contract with a professional team. My memories are skewered by emotional highs juxtaposed with physical lows. I can still make my hands sweat remembering breakneck descents in the pouring rain and spectacular Pyrénéen mountain vistas. But these recollections are, in many ways, the highlights. The racing cyclist lives a monastic existence. Train, eat, sleep, repeat.

One memory from my first season of full-time racing stands out for me. I'd discovered an interest in nutrition. My knowledge was scant, but I'd devised a dietary programme that combined various powders and gels, which I was hopeful would enhance my performance.

I settled into the team car for the journey down to Perpignan, bidon (bike bottle) at my side, ready to top-off my muscle glycogen stores at the perfect time before the first brutal effort of the year. After a few of hours driving, the Director Sportif announced that we would be making a stop. I expected the pause to be brief, but a curious scene began to unfold. At a leisurely pace, staff and riders began to unpack the van. Coolers were opened, a couple of picnic tables appeared. The soigneur arrived with an armful of baguettes, buttering them with a skill that only comes through years of experience. Thermos flasks were unsealed and steaming pasta poured onto the plates. Supermarket ham was quickly sliced into the mix. Next, I heard the "pop" of a cork as small plastic glasses were charged with what appeared to be an entirely palatable Minervois.

"Where eeez your fud, Jemz?" the one English speaking rider on my team enquired. I stared at my bottle of carbohydrate and branched chain amino acids, and gave it a shake in the vain hope of breaking down the sediment that was gathering at the bottom. I sipped sullenly on the mixture, as my teammates stared at me uncomprehendingly.

It was the beginning of a cultural cross-pollination process that continued throughout my cycling career. The old and new worlds of cycling can learn from each other. Perhaps pasta isn't the optimum pre-race fuel, but likewise, my liquid meal probably had room for improvement.

Over the course of the following seasons I found myself asking questions about nutrition and other aspects of the sport. Staring at my heart rate monitor and noting its variability made me wonder whether there were better ways to gauge training effort and track improvement. Pedalling for thousands of miles with the saddle raised as high as possible and the stem 'slammed', as was the custom, made me query whether there was a more scientific means of connecting the rider with their equipment. I saw myself as a researcher and my body as a living experiment.

When my dreams of cycling superstardom sank, I continued my quest to improve cycling performance by studying Sports Science. More than ten years on, I continue to experiment on myself, but at Cyclefit UK, I also work with other cyclists, both amateurs and professionals, helping them make the most of the science of the sport. I look back on my racing days with fondness and a hint of regret. I should have joined them with a glass of red that day.

CYCLING JARGON

Bidon A water bottle

Blow Up Someone who has gone into oxygen deficit and can no longer keep up with the riders around them.

Bonk To bonk is to hit the wall. A depletion of glycogen in the muscles from not being properly fueled.

Broom Wagon A vehicle that follows a race carrying equipment and collecting the riders that are unable to complete the course.

Cadence The rate at which a cyclist pedals.

Clincher A standard tyre with a separate inner tube.

Criterium A short, multi-lap course ranging from 800m to 5km. It is a mass start event and often takes place in city centres.

Classics Series of one-day races, most notably Milan-San Remo, Tour of Flanders, Gent-Wevelgem, Paris-Roubaix, Fléche Wallonne and the Tour of Lombardy.

Col French for mountain pass.

Directeur Sportif The manager of a cycling team. They will follow the race in a team car and communicate with the riders en route.

Domestique A rider whose job it is to work for his teammates, and in particular the leader of the team. He will get food and water from the team cars, and if needs be, sacrifice a wheel or bike.

Drops The lower part of the handlebars.

Dropped To be unable to keep up and to get left behind by the group or peloton.

Echelon A line of riders drafting diagonally as close as possible in a crosswind.

Étape A stage in a multi-day road race.

Flamme Rouge A red flag over the road marking the final kilometre of a race.

General Classification (GC) The overall standings in a stage race. If a rider is a GC rider he is aiming for a podium position at the end of a stage race.

Giro The Giro d'Italia. One of the three 'grand tours'. A three week stage race in Italy. Takes place in May.

Hammer To ride is hard is also referred to as 'putting the hammer down'.

Hors Catégorie (HC) A climb that is beyond category. There are generally 4 categories in a stage race, from 4 (the easiest) to 1 (hard). HC is really hard.

Individual Time Trial (ITT) A race against the clock. Riders set off at timed intervals and cannot draft one another at any stage.

Lantern Rouge The rider who finishes last in the GC at the end of a stage race.

Laughing Group A group of riders who are only aiming to complete the race, not contest the finish.

Lead Out A technique used by sprinters, whereby a rider accelerates as fast as he can with the sprinter sheltering in his slipstream, and when the rider